EMPTY HOTEL ROOMS MEANT FOR US

CHRISTINA HART

EMPTY HOTEL ROOMS MEANT FOR US

ISBN-13: 978-1519414267
ISBN-10: 1519414269

For the few men I've loved –
I still carry pieces of you with me.

LIKE ROPES

There were men.
Of course there
were men –
men like the neon lights
out front of the bar,
men like the rope
I'd choose to
hang myself with,
men like the calming vanilla
I'd add to my coffee,
men who would make me
question if there really
only was one Highlander,
men who would make me
question everything,
men who used me,
men who worshipped me,
men who loved me.

PUSHING CARTS

I will take these parts of you
and push this fucking cart
around town until you try
to come take them back.
But you won't –
you always loved being lost.

PIECES OF YOU IN MY POCKET

You wrote two
little words on a
crumpled piece
of paper and
stuck it in my
jacket pocket
three years ago.
I found it
a few days later.
It said
"Hello beautiful."
I still have it.
And even when
I'm not wearing
that jacket,
my pockets
are always full
of pieces of you.

POKING HOLES

I grew tired of
blowing dandelion fuzz,
wishing you'd come back to me.
I got sick of
thinking about the
way you used to
drift off to sleep
and smile with
your eyes still closed
when I'd try to
keep you awake.
The mistakes I made –
with you – they like to
hang around and
remind me of all the ways
I poked holes in this thing
until it started to sink.
But the hope?
The hope I still have
for us is probably
the worst of it all.
Yet somehow
it feels good,
and right now,
I don't think
I'll ever tire of it.
That hope is probably
the only thing

that's keeping me afloat.

I KNEW YOU ONCE

I never knew much
to brag about.
I could never carry
on a conversation
on worldly or
scientific things –
but I knew you once.
I knew you then
and I like to think
I still know you now.
I knew that you
liked magic –
like that one time
after we
first broke up when
you came to visit me
at work to tell me
you missed me and
you pulled my favorite
kind of milkshake
out of your pocket.
I didn't know how
you did it but I knew
you meant to make me
smile.
I knew you loved
music. I knew you'd
make it one day, with

or without me by
your side. I knew
your voice, when
you talked and when
you sang and whispered
and laughed. I knew it was
the most beautiful sound I'd
ever heard, and whether you
were singing or not
it all sounded like
music to me.
I knew your journal.
I wrote in it when I would
help you write lyrics to
your songs. I knew your
handwriting. I knew your
eyes and the way they'd
look back at me in the
same way mine were
looking at you.
I knew you wanted to
get a dog again, like the
one you used to have
before things went dim.
I knew you were a
recovering heroin addict but
I knew you were so much
more than that.
I know you're in Texas now
but tell me, did you ever get
another dog? Do your eyes
look back at another girl

the way they used to
look at me? Do you still
have that journal? Did you
ever finish that song we
started writing together?
Just tell me something.
Tell me anything.
You could tell me
you hate me and
I'd sit there and
listen.
Go on.
My ears are all yours.

DISMEMBERING LOVERS

There are a million ways
to kill someone
that leaves them
able to walk away.

NEVER ENOUGH

My manuscript sat on your
nightstand collecting dust
for almost a year and you
liked to say you were in
love with an author but you
never tried to fall in love
with my words and if
they weren't enough for
you then what makes me
think they'll be enough
for you now?

ROMANCE NOVELS

That's the problem with
writers —
it's impossible for us to
forget the lovers we
still have romance novels
written inside of us for
even though they've
become tragedies.

SCRIBBLING YOUR NAME

I could scribble your name
a thousand times and it
wouldn't mean a damn thing
unless you gave me the
chance to show you.

DARK LIGHTS

I see glimpses of you
in the air, at the bar,
at the store. I see
flashes of you
even when my
eyes are open, glued
to the television
to distract me from
the fact that you are
not sitting beside me.
I cannot stand the
cold, dead darkness of
an empty room.
I need to keep the
lights on and pretend
you'll turn them off
when you come
back to bed.

BURNING BRIDGES

I'm afraid of bridges –
afraid of crossing them,
afraid of burning them,
afraid of taking the wheel
and spinning it until I
veer straight off the side
of them.
But most of all,
I'm afraid I'll never find
the one that
leads me back
to you.

HAIR IN FISTS

You always liked
my hair long, and
so did I. But now,
I don't know
if I'll ever cut it and
I don't know if it's
for you or for me.
But I remember your
hands in it – the way you
used to wrap it around
your fist, the way you'd
try to brush out the
knots with your fingers,
the way you'd find strands
of it around your apartment,
the way you'd tell me
not to cut it whenever
I got sick of the weight.
I always liked my hair
long. But maybe now
I keep it for you
even though you're gone.
But I can't use that
conditioner anymore –
the one you used to
stop me for, just so you
could smell it. I can't.
But I still wear our favorite perfume.

15

YOU, ME, AND THE MOON

Most of the nights
we spent together
were just you, me,
and the moon.
And she had her
hands full with us
even when she wasn't.
The stars beside her
have kept our
secrets for years.
Sometimes I wonder
if they ever thought
we'd make it –
I still can't bring
myself to tell them
that we didn't.

CHEAP WISHES

What a tragedy it is —
all this love I still
have for you, just
wasting away inside
my chest.
It could be
worth so much more
to someone who
wanted it.
If I could bottle
it up, I'd sell it at
a garage sale for
50 cents. And I'd
take that change
and toss it into a
well, hoping you
would somehow
hear me for the
last time.
But then again,
I always waste my
wishes on the
impossible.

BLOWING LIDS

The tea kettle
goes off
in the morning
and I wonder
if I'd blow my
own lid too
if given the
opportunity.

SUNDAYS AT ROSE'S

Remember those Sunday mornings
we spent at Rose's?
We'd order banana pancakes
and sit next to each other
in the booth but even
holding hands,
arms and legs touching,
we were never close enough.
It was never enough –
even when we were
tangled up in
each other in ways
that only you and I
would ever know of.

QUIET WALKS OFF MAIN STREET

I never know where I am
or what this life is
but I know sometimes
it's a quiet walk
off Main Street and a pack
of Marlboro Menthol Lights
to myself and a bottle
no one tells me to
put down to
watch the sunrise
instead.

HEARTBURN

Was it wrong that
I dreamed of him?
Was it wrong that
I often thought about
what it would be like?
If we touched?
If we held each other
like the world had
just caught fire? If he
kissed me like he was
trying to make me
shut the fuck up
for once? If we held
hands just one time to see
that spark of skin and
sin that I've been
warned of?
I want to give him
Advil for this headache
and Tums for this
heartburn but is it wrong
that I want to give him
anything at all?

TAILSPIN

I swear, if we let
ourselves, we'd
fucking take this town
and tailspin it all into
turmoil but together
we would be far
more dangerous than
perhaps even you or I
could handle.
If fate allowed it,
we'd have corrupted
a hell of a lot more
than sins of desire.
If we touched,
we'd have alluded to
conspire something more
than this regret of
never allowing ourselves
to touch
at all.

SKIP THE SHEEP

There was something about
his tired raspy voice just
before he'd fall asleep
that made me pray he'd
give up counting his sheep
tonight so just this once
he could dream of me
instead.

FAMILIAR HANDS

His hands never ran
along any part of me,
but they were not foreign.
No, I've dreamed of
them so often that they've
become familiar.
And it was ironic
how his hands
never touched me
but I can still
feel them
all
over
me.

EMPTY HOTEL ROOMS MEANT FOR US

I think about what
it would be like –
leaving the hotel room
in complete disarray. I'd make
them leave your favorite
chocolate on the pillow and
my handprints across your
chest. I'd order a lifetime
of regrets to stamp upon
your heart and a million
reasons as to why
this was wrong
but mainly, I'd order a
bouquet of dead flowers
for my condolences that
we were never allowed
to be together
at the right time.

CHRISTINA HART

JUST KEEP SWIMMING

Some days I had dreams
about us —
but most of the time
it was me, fighting
against that intangible
current, swimming like hell
to the shoreline so
I could pretend we were
never lost at sea
at all.

WILD THINGS

There are times
I wonder about
life and men and
love and dreams –
are any of them
real?

HUMANITY IN WALMART

Something happened in
that store
when all the carts
were gone
and I carried that
28 pack of Poland Spring
across Walmart like
I was going to war.
And when I got to
the checkout counter
I asked a stranger to
pull my wallet out of
my armpit and he looked
confused but I said
please and he did
and it was awkward but
I thought,
this –
this is humanity –
this is what it's all about.

WHAT'S LEFT OF THIS HEART

I like to feed
the ghosts
of my past.
They're hungry.
They're always
hungry.
And whatever's
left of this
heart never
seems to be
enough to
satisfy them.

WHAT FEELINGS?

Most of my feelings
broke a long time ago
but there are some left
that take just the
right kind of wrong
person to snap them
in half like twigs
from a beautiful
rotting tree –
and even then
I don't think
they will make a
single sound.

THEM AND HIM

I always fall in love
with men who are
just as uncontrollable
and wild as me –
the type of men who
cannot be tamed,
the type of men
who step in dog
shit and keep walking,
the type of men with
dirty white t-shirts
who sit on broken
chairs, wanting to
try it just to see
how long it takes
before it all gives
out from right
underneath them.

LOVE IN WAVES

I love in patterns
and colors not
meant for
anyone
ordinary
or sane.

THE DARK PRETTY THINGS

I never cared
about the light
in someone's eyes.
For me,
it was always
about the
dark pretty things
behind them.

GRAVE ANGELS

One year I think
there will be a winter here
that buries us all beneath
the snow and I'd like
to see who cares enough
to try to make it out
alive and how many
of us choose to stay
under there
making snow angels until
the coldness sets
in to freeze us
there in our hidden
white graves.

BACK ALLEY

There's a back alley
somewhere between
here and now and
tomorrow, a path
that might just
lead you home if
you're brave enough
to risk it.
Streetlights are your
best bet before you
take that first step.
But keep going –
you won't recognize
light until you've known
complete and utter
darkness.

WITHOUT WORDS

There were a few men
who spoke to me
without ever saying a
word. Sometimes they
screamed my name –
other times it was
only a whisper, a look or
a smile that told me
they wanted to tell me so
much more and I wonder
how I occasionally think of
them and miss them
without ever hearing the
sound of their voice.

SCREWS OF YOU

There's a man out there
who has hands strong
enough to handle me and
enough patience to try –
I know because I loved
him like the seasons would
never change but eventually
the leaves fell and the
flowers dried up and
the snow fell, burying
everything we worked
so hard to build
and at times I try to piece
it all back together but
I'm missing all the screws
that belong to you.

I MEANT IT

And it sounds cliché
but when I told you
I loved you
I meant it –
but what
I really meant
was that I'd destroy
everything in this
world for you,
including myself.

DREAMER

I guess that
sometimes
I'm a hopeless
fucking romantic
because of you
and the way you
say my name
even though it
will never be heard
in all the ways you
say it even when
I'm not around.

I WANTED THEM TO KNOW

Before it all ended
before it began
I wanted to make
someone cry.
I wanted the
salty reminder
left with someone
other than me
of exactly what
this all is.
I wanted them to
be alone with
how I felt about
him then and how I
feel about you now.
I wanted them
to sit down with
you for five minutes,
not even a foot apart,
and I wanted them to
know that they
couldn't touch you
or hold you or
tell you how much
they fucking love
you and wish you'd
come a little closer.
I wanted them to

grasp just how
hard it is to look
at you and
know it was all
an impossible dream.
I wanted them to
know how I want
to take your hand
and hold it for just
one minute. I wanted
them to know how
your eyes haunt me
even when I'm alone.
I wanted them to
know that I'm a
terrible person for
wanting things I
can't want.
I wanted them
to know that
when "New York
State of Mind" comes on
I think of you and
that when anything
comes on I think of
you. I wanted them to
know what it was like
to know they could never
have you. I wanted them
to know what it was
like to love you.

Made in the USA
Middletown, DE
06 February 2017